FOREIGN NATIONAL

Also by Laurence Hutchman

The Twilight Kingdom
Explorations
Blue Riders

FOREIGN NATIONAL

Laurence Hutchman

For Carmelo
more poems
about immigrants
all all best

Laurence Hutchman

AGAWA PRESS

October 2, 2013

1993

Poems have previously appeared in: *The Antigonish Review, Blue Buffalo, Canadian Literature, CV II, Garden Varieties, The Lyric Paragraph, Northern Light, The Northern Line, Poetry Toronto, Prism, Wayzegoose, Zymergy.*

Many people assisted in the production of this work. The author thanks Brian Bartlett, Ronnie Brown, Charlotte Hussey and Heather Ferguson for their support and advice, and Colin Morton, Maria Jacobs, Yiota Karaiskos and Sylvia Adams for reading the text. Darcy Moorey, Collections Manager of the Canada Council Art Bank, was both helpful and courteous, and Geoff Todd of Hignell Printing demonstrated exceptional patience, flexibility and professionalism. Luc Bourgie provided impeccable layout under very tight deadlines. Finally, special thanks go to Hugh Hood for his encouragement and insight.

Cover illustration: Correspondence #1
    by Al Neil, Vancouver, British Columbia
    Collection of the Canada Council Art Bank /
    Collection de la Banque d'oeuvres d'art du
        Conseil des Arts du Canada
Art photography: Justin Wonnacott, Ottawa, Ontario
Author's photo: Guy Lebel, St. Basile, New Brunswick
Layout and cover design: Luc Bourgie, Hull, Quebec
Printing: Hignell Printing Limited, Winnipeg, Manitoba

Canadian Cataloguing in Publication Data
Hutchman, Laurence
    Foreign National
Poems.
ISBN 0-9693976-4-X
    I. Title
PS8565.U83F67 1993   C811'.54   C94-900041-8
PR9199.3.H88F67 1993

Agawa Press
P.O. Box 807, Station B
Ottawa, Ontario
Canada K1P 5P9

for Mary

CONTENTS

BURNT ISLAND LAKE

DARK WINDOWS

Dream of Origins

I wake up and see the headlines:
science has discovered God.
A scientist has probed and found
particles of radiation,
the origins of the universe rippling
on a distant primordial shore.
I look upon the blue and pink shell —
the genesis of all we know.
This morning in the elegant hotel room
the children, as usual, scramble over the bed.

I am always searching for the beginning:
in the stroller watching the orange sky
through black tangled branches,
in the playhouse looking at the excited eyes
of birds, wondering how I am like them.

I dream of going back to Ireland after the war
to rescue Granny's relics.
Father says, "You should search the photos
to get the whole picture:"
George and I playing hockey with potato sack nets,
the mad minister, the puritan boarders,
the old fishermen who returned,
the young soldiers who did not.

You cannot deny them.
You must not miss the plane.
You must take your family with you,
gather them all into your history of Edenmore Street.

We are always looking for that beginning,
that first moment we mouth our names
and know them as ourselves,
when we hear our voices and know they are us,
when history comes out of the photos.
It is then we cry out against
bruised skin, broken windows, blind vision.

It is then we travel through the dark morning,
gaze from the edge at the beginning:
in the dark sea of space,
in the distant, intimate matrix,
the blue and pink celestial shell.
And in the suspended
silent whirr we listen for voices,
the unacknowledged families,
                    so many unending stars...

FAMILY LINES

Lost Language

Photo albums span the decades:
wartime, marriage, early years in Canada.
The sounds of Dutch swell within me,
a child's language
until I know them again.

I read a language I knew and forgot —
"j's" and "t's" and Dutch diphthongs
(how I was ashamed of those comic vowels).
Sounds rise and break in me
sibilance of sea, rush of waves,
Scheveningen, Katwijk, Noordwijk...

Sounds ripen in the mouth:
beschuit, pindakaas, boterham
sinaasappel...lekker... ahh... a language of violets,
orchids, solariums and that tobacco...

The words break in me
touching the page they dissolve the lines
of my mother's white handwriting —
change into weather, the lonely
excitement of windy beaches,
seagrass, kelp, the briny smell
blowing the waking coldness off
Scheveningen, Katwijk, Noordwijk...

Plane Vision

Thirty-five thousand feet up
looking at myself reading a page
from out there in the clouds and stars...
watching the page grow slowly
in the oval darkness, becoming
a sculptured and Biblical book.
These pages are unknown characters.
Beyond the humming darkness
is another page and still another.
These are my separate selves.
These are the pages of my life,
my father's, my grandfather's.
Do not forget my mother's life, my grandmother's
(the Dutch girl within the girl)
each page shining in the distance.
I transcribe the pages until they become
the voices of my family.
My hand extends through the clouds
encompasses the veiled hills of my history.

The Garden

1

That summer before we came to Canada
we walked among tents
where *meisjes* sold fish
and old men swallowed herring:
I ate *stroopwafels* and twirled a pinwheel.
Above Wassenaar the arms of the windmill whirred.

Mother guided me by the lake
where swans glided past the palace,
by the sphinx-lions
and over the arched wooden bridge:
the angel rose in a Biblical vision,
her eyes looked upward
    vibrant wings spread on the air.

2

So I approach you again
your wings tarnished, yet graceful.
Along this road Panzer divisions
rolled in to occupy the country.
Here Herman sneaked out
to gather firewood
under your watchful eye.
V 2's whistled overhead,
destroyed cities in England.

By the pond we walk
where parents hid in the tall grass
spying on Opa and Oma, strolling.
They were married in that city hall —
that childhood palace. Now the mayor
and his councillors pass bylaws
under chandeliers. We cross
the bridge above the sleeping swans.

In that cottage an artist and his wife
draw the magic of colour on white space,
colour wild as animals and flowers
drawing a new geometry
            perhaps an image of you.

    3

Angel, I recall you
on monuments, gravestones, mountains;
in mornings before school I saw you
on the Dutch war plaque,
in Herman's house at dawn
when the light
            broke through the curtains
falling on Athena
                broke through the leaves
into song
            above the milling streets
of business.

At twilight this park is a genesis.
We move through the shadows,
leave the cities in war;
night comes rustling
in the leaves
            and the fountain rises,
mingles with our voices
            breaking into colour
over the dark water.

Encounters with History

My parents spoke about their meetings with history,
father walking through the ruins of Hamburg
to the lonely lights of the cinema: "A Brief Encounter."

Mother spoke of the Rhineland hotel in 1933
the drunken soldiers, the waving of flags.
Her girlfriend said, "You want to see the old man's room?"
Pushing open the door they saw the big black eagle
rise over the unmade bed where Hitler slept.

After the war in the flag-happy streets
of the Hague, she waved at Churchill
his fingers raised in the V sign
as he passed in the black limousine.

For many years they kept these stories
to themselves. Father speaks of the time
before the war when he was nine
running along the Donegal hills
after Amelia Earhart's plane.
She blew him a kiss
before disappearing forever.

Opa

Five years old I stare up at him
mountainous, in the white wicker chair
puffing a Havana among the gardenias.
His hard blue eyes gaze through smoke
as his stained fingers reach for a deck of cards...

He captained cargoes through risky waters
watched ships founder and people drown
in the *Zuiderzee*. He made a fortune:
Russian railways, German marks, South African mines —
lost it all in the Depression.

The Rhineland in the thirties
drunken soldiers raised swastikas on jeeps.
Opa knew war was in the wind,
refused to deal with infiltrators.
The night Rotterdam was bombed
he cycled from Wassenaar to see his houses razed,
then turned and rode home.

Always danger. In the darkened attic
he listened on headphones to BBC reports,
while below teenage daughters
listened to blue-eyed Sinatra;
love songs echoed through the occupied land.
In his eighties still
he skated the long canals with his sons.

Dinner is a late night ritual.
Opa stares at me eating dessert too quickly.
Later in the solarium he takes the deck
delicately, in stiff, stained fingers
lifts each king, queen, knight,
places them beside each other, making
the walls and ceilings rise
into a blue and white house.

Work Camp

— for Robert Veldhuisen

After the bombing of Rotterdam that was it.
Opa and you cycle through the flaming streets
past streaming refugees. There are new laws.
Jews vanish. An edict summons boys from villages.
When the commandant comes to the *Hoflaan*,
you are on the soccer field.

On the station platform your family
is frozen in grief. You stick with friends.
Familiar water fades into alien country,
the Black Forest. Behind barbed wire
you sew uniforms long into the night.
Soccer on Sundays is the only freedom.
After months letters come less often.
Life is machines, uniforms, barbed wire sky.
A friend tries to escape, is shipped to Auschwitz.
At night planes drone overhead. You wait, listen.
One morning the compound is deserted
                    and the gate open...

You return to flags, parades, welcome lines.
You are treated as a traitor.
Your son will not go into the army.

Frank

I sit in the Billy Bishop Legion in Vancouver
with a cousin I haven't seen in five years.
He is a media agent with a local TV station,
owns a ski resort and is president of a golf club.
"Been a while since we've seen you, Frank,"
the bartender calls.

He speaks about growing up lonely as a boy,
speaks of the other boys with families:
"I regretted... resented the absence of family
and so looked to *them*."
He recalls Uncle Freddy, all-star pilot,
and the others who defended the skies
in the Battle of Britain. We sit among
regiment mottos, animal masks,
the British colonel like a war movie star.

On the wall is a painting of a Lancaster at twilight:
eleven men on the moist expectant tarmac,
standing under the huge throbbing beast.
The night is shot through with smoky light
the plane revving — perhaps for the last mission
flying through the void against an enemy
much like yourself,
            awaiting battle and decision.

"I remember one night," he says.
"My father and mother sent me away to a movie.
I knew something was up. I was with a friend.
I kept looking up into the light, pretending
the light was making my eyes blink."

His eyes don't look at me,
but up at that same bright light.
His eyes hold rings of light in darkness:
"It was New Year's 1943 when we heard.
He was killed by a Spandau at Ortono."

From the dark Legion beyond the pictures
the men and women loudly talk,
a wild Ulsterman belts out this song.
Time to leave. The big Lancaster idles
for its final flight.
            The men huddle on the wet runway
smoke, joke and talk about women,
not looking to anything, only a memory
but listening to the throbbing
as if it were your heart.
Now, he's off.

I read the motto of his father's regiment
with the eagle on his cap.
In the glass case, the soldier's prayer,
Teach us the way that we should die.

Elegy for Sarah

Born under the pagan ring where cold sun radiates
over the rough, spilling waters of Lough Swilly,
where the Earls, exiled from Ulster, sailed
for Europe. As a girl you watched the stormy shore, struggled
with a father's control; you forged a glowing kindness,
stoked the fire in the cold air that blew down from Scalp.

Three times I climbed the Celtic mount,
searched the hills for your place of birth
lost in the ridges and rumours of mountains,
the sudden streams. Through the rusty heather,
wind blows clearly as your voice. To the pagan
ring of Grianan, I climbed and looked down
on the border to the lumbering of war machinery.

Christmas morning the train glided along the seashore
toward you in that little home hollowed
out of rock and plaster at the end of Edenmore Street.
Beside grandfather in the great oak bed
you raised your eyes to the frightened child,
who saw your eyes clearly in the lamplight.
Now, in another country, I descend the stairs.
I hear your death in the wind's pause over dark ice.

Grandmother, Sarah, white light falls across the mountain
through the clouds and the shadow of the picture.
I see you on a windy day as a girl scrambling
over the waving heather on Grianan's dark flanks.
You were never younger than grandmother
yet in the oval photograph with two sons
on your knee, you are a heroine
in a Dickens' novel, or from the silent screen.

At the edge of the scullery you stood,
a Catholic woman in a house of Protestant men,
and made this border the centre.
You served the eccentric minister with patience,
"Him, with the dog collar going into the bookies,
who yammed, girned and growsed."
You carried your belief quietly as a stone cross
firmly lined against the palm of your hand.

Sarah, you are gone; and you joked that if I came back
you were going to Grianan, and now I search
for you along those Irish border slopes
where you once waited for Freddy
to come back from the mists of the Somme,
or waited to see his bicycle with the miner's lamp
wind slowly down the crossing.

The earth is white and empty of your presence:
river, pines, house still in a different world.
You now lie overlooking the Brandywell
beyond the games, spires and war.
I can only say how much your silence holds,
how it holds me in your own strong sway.

Woman in the Well

Adrian,
they said you were in prison
but you weren't.
Across the crackling fire you speak,
    "Allison, she's a big woman,
        not many like her.
    There, by the house, she was walk'n."
You raise a hand across flames.
    "I don't know how
        but she falls over a stone
    down into the well
              an' we can hear her yell'n.

We wander over an' calls down,
'Are you ok?'
              an' she starts a yell'n an' holler'n
as if somethin's wrong with her
    splash'n down there like some big catfish woman
thrash'n about there
        like a whale.

Why you good-for-nothing bastards,
can't you do anything to help a woman?
An' we begin wander'n across the field
  an' gets a big hook
it bein' sharp as a harpoon.

26

An' we says,
'Watch out, we're throw'n it down.'
All we hear's a splash an' a yell.
   An' she's got the line
an' we're hugg'n an' heav'n
draw'n her up
            an' she's like some heavy fish
an' we're pull'n it across the field.

And then
        there she is,
            glistn'n like some fish woman,
        like you never seen
            that woman angry
                    com'n toward us."

The Farm

1

Away from the retirement party
I wander across windy fields
before the open rolling hills and shoaled clouds.
Your grandfather lived at the edge
among these tools and machines:
the cultivator, binder, sower and democrat.

Stand among the barn ruins
the home of your grandfather.
Did he not rescue the children, driving horses
across the ice until they were safe on shore,
then danced the night away —
the best dancer for miles around.
Still they sing his songs at parties.

Year by year he pushed back the borders of the farm;
the crops were difficult
        and the children came.
In these ravines and on hillsides you see the cairns,
monuments to his will, his testament.

The only way to cross these fields is to follow
the paths of cows. I wander at the edge of ruins
trace the rotting fences of your grandmother's garden;
the old wagon wheels are a civil war scene,
family machines rusting back into earth.

Inside the liquor flows freely as the arguments:
relatives are on the edge of violence.
Women slip into the winter kitchen
for a drink, while reformed men struggle
to stay on the wagon.
When your grandmother died
they tore the house apart fighting
over radios and rosaries.

In 1953 Edward harvested the last field
by Philips' line, put down his plow
and made the long trek
down the hills to the waiting farmhouse,
said "that's enough" to your grandmother,
left for Hamilton the next day.

2

Morning, the bed is a boat,
gliding through dawn mists.
In amber light I trace wallpaper patterns
until they become a genealogical map,
capillaries intersecting with concession lines.

The house has been here so long
the stain composes lost faces.
The pictures: faded British caricatures
Jesus, an old Irish patriarch
Mary, sad mother of Connemara
waiting for the return of her fishermen.

These voices rise through the summer kitchen pipe,
voices blurred by smoke and bird calls.
Voices of grandmother, great grandparents
trailing off into the lives of first arrivals.
Follow the music through my fingers
into the first sunlight, as the ship sails
into the St. Lawrence, past the Quebec citadel.
Follow the river among the gold gleaming islands
to the quiet shores of Prince Edward County
north to this rocky land.

Roots Among the Rocks

1

Beneath the wheels the stones roll
as we glide through fields
where granite rocks are gods —
on the fence that thorned figure Ixion
nailed to his spinning wheel.
Through the blood-coned sumac
and the Indian grove we drive
where your mother hummed tunes
from the big band era between battle news.

Bridge clatters and another board splinters,
Dutch elms withering over rough road.
By the field's edge an old trunk decays.
The Irish immigrated to Hastings,
divided the loyalist lines into a miniature homeland:
Marmora, Wicklow, Dungannon.
They fought until that afternoon in Lonsdale
when a shot from the crowd brought
proud Winters down and the murderers
slipped across the bay to Syracuse or Oswego.
Whatever was in those letters was burned in the barn.

Your grandfather, Arthur, bard of the fields,
was five then. For years he wandered Hastings County.
How many lovers had he in the woods
until, at the age of fifty, after his mother's death
he married a girl twenty-five years his junior.

2

Each room you read like a page from a book:
bleeding valentine hearts of Jesus hang over doorways,
the uncertain stairs lead to dark bedrooms,
the wooden wheelchair your invalid grandmother
rocked in until her grave.

These roots grow wild among the rocks,
rumours rustle through the bulrushes,
incense rises from Joseph and Mary
yet you, grandfather, jangled your jigs
from the harmonica, thumping floorboards,
magnetizing children with moonstruck eyes
while grandmother peeled potatoes,
watched the road rise and fall like a sigh.
Malice shimmered in the blood-red brook
flowed out under the oblivion of a winter moon.

During the war years your mother worked
in the Bristol aircraft plant, crossed
concession lines to marry your Protestant father
who, enlisting for service, got not further than B.C.
where he learned to ski and polish the colonel's car,
but another uncle, Ross, entered the Gerry Blitz
returned to waken nights, aim a rifle at his mother's eyes.

Your sister dead in her seventeenth year.
Handicapped, she opened your lives;
her lips formed imperfect words,
what light her eyes held.

3

Now that night is coming on
the stream is a vessel
reflecting the still clouds
as it flows around banks
by broken wheels, rusty tools.
An abandoned plow lies
half-buried in the mud.

Before this window
you embrace me as I write these words —
soft bevel of your breasts touches my body,
light touches golden crest of the slope
touched with the last light of the still mist.

We are alone while the others are at church.
Soon our bodies will meet.
Stream flows through the banks;
the herd is quiet in the ruined barn.
Crickets chirp as stars appear
and you settle in a red chair,
slip pink earring shells
into the velvet case of darkness.

A CHILD'S HISTORY OF STAMPS

Trunks

Oom Adriaan, prisoner of war, left Indonesia
with the trunks. They carry our possessions
to Canada and serve as tables and dressers.
Lifeboats, they sit beside the furnace,
mother's last tie to Europe.

She holds onto them as her history,
warns us of the valuables they contain.
Year after year they float in dusty motes
of violet sunbars like family crypts,
Egyptian sarcophagi at the ROM.

We lug one down, open the lid to the smell of Opa,
aroma of Havana cigars on his suits and shoes,
maybe a few Dutch guilders or dominoes jingle
in his pockets. Further down we find
the black bordered envelopes,
the orange cameo, Queen Juliana,
the foreign diseases and deaths,
the tears of fury on rainy afternoons.

They survive father's clean up purges, hockey shoot-outs,
weekend arguments. One day searching for stamps
they become treasure chests as George and I
forage through possessions, searching for
the British Guyana stamp and discover
the rare stamp of the blue-sceptred queen
who ruled the kingdom of *Helvetia*.
These stamps would make us rich!

We dig down through the years of photos:
bombed bridges, downed planes, Irish honeymoon shots —
down through chiffon party gowns,
polka dot maternity dresses to the chest bottom:
a passport and rows of stamps.
Up the stairs we scramble, ask mother to decipher the codes.
She speaks of lining up for rations: bread, sugar, tea.

She opens up the passport of her lost country.
"I've been looking for this for years,"
(her picture, curly-haired girl —
Ingrid Bergman, the lost princess).
"Can we have these stamps?"
"No," she clutches the bouquet to her breast.
"I need these," as if she plans to sail for Holland
tomorrow, and this is the last ticket.

A Child's History of Stamps

I learned to handle the stamps as carefully
as the newborn baby, cradling their edges.
More than any encyclopedia
this was the gateway to the world.
Through telescopic windows I looked into
lush tropical countries: flowers, lions, butterflies,
Olympic runners caught in still motion.
    For the first time I saw Hitler — no Frankenstein —
but a man with a mustache, and the Spanish General whose
bald skull shone like a fierce moon, half-man, half-beast.
The English kings were cameos, white busts on mantelpieces.
Yet it was not the faces, but the politics of stamps:
the Hungarian Revolution painted
on faded brown cloth, blood staining the print.
Whose tormented hands had it passed through?
I could hardly read its smudged lines,
peasants rising against the king's throne.
Each stamp a different war scene
— death, suffering and victory.

First Desk

Late night waking, the sandalwood desk
moored like Opa's old sea chest.
The lost bureau is open once more
and my treasures are within its drawers:
the polished mother-of-pearl knife,
hundreds of coins from my *Globe and Mail* route.

Where did that desk go?
The Beehive NHL All Star autographed photos,
the Bible with its pale illustrations of miracles,
Genesis with the red apple of sin
next to eternal Archie, forever Jughead.
Where is the archive of trading cards:
labyrinth, puzzle, World War II
(Pearl Harbour, Iwo Jima),
the aroma of gum rising from generations
of American and National League baseball stars?

Where did that desk come from?
His face comes back to me,
rises from strange suburban shades,
the high school student with brush cut and glasses
who one day, one restless Sunday
left the semi-detached life of our subdivision
for an unknown destination.
He left this desk and his books:
Pauline Johnson, dipping her rhyme in the wilderness,
a pre-war reader with trains and planes,
A New Heaven and a New Earth,
the future already long gone.

Where is that desk?
— Gone along with the cards,
the comics, the hockey pads, my red glider,
just gone when we moved
and nothing came with us.
I didn't even notice, not until now,
my first golden desk
in the darkness, waiting...

Kaleidoscope

Christmas morning and I am seven
I hold the kaleidoscope for the first time;
patterns change as exotic tapestries blossom
into orchids, violets and roses.
Beyond the shores of waking I travel
past blue suns to orange planets,
gardens and menageries. I turn
the dream glass in my fingers
and things turn into one another:
silver dulcimers, red diamonds, sapphire waves.
I see myself in the old brick house:
relatives, presents, flowers and tangerines.
I see the illuminated fir, the winding road,
the little church, the river,
and the blue-gold earth, turning.

Fall of the House of Orange

In the centre of our living room table
the plate of the House of Orange
(the Prince and Princess surrounded by *sinaasappels*)
gathers in letters, coins and keys.
Father broke plates Sunday afternoons,
but did not touch this one.

He sewed the siege crest on his breast pocket.
The skeleton sits on the rock,
death's white gleaming twin.
How proudly he wears that blazer
commemorating thirteen starving boys
who ate boots until
William of Orange landed on the Irish shore.

Orangeman, "What can I do with a woman who gives
me an orange every day of my life for twenty-five years
when she knows I hate oranges?"
"Where is the William of Orange plate?" I ask.
"It's upstairs in two pieces in your mother's bedroom."

I stand in the still Dutch room.
Out of the plastic Hudson's Bay bag
I handle the plate
piece by piece:
mother dabs the cheek of the wounded soldier,
Robert stitches Nazi uniforms
in the Black Forest, Opa grips the handlebars
and watches Rotterdam burn.

I sift ceramic petals —
the fallen House of Orange.
These pieces are words lost.
I cannot put this plate
together, too many pieces missing.
Mother enters the room.

"What does this motto mean?"
Gehoont   Gesmaat   Gesart

She murmurs,
"scorned... reviled... tormented..."

The Fathers

The fathers of our streets were quiet
when they weren't working or drinking
until they broke out in rage against their sons.
Brian acted out the Howdy Doody puppet show;
his father brooded among his stamps like a dictator,
then kicked us out into the cold spring air.

Billy let us play in the loft of his barn
and we climbed up to a diving platform
jumping and gliding into engulfing straw.
In the Victorian dining room his father shouted,
"How many times have I told you not to disturb the animals?"
His hands shook the doilies, teacups, porcelain dolls,
spun Billy across the floor where he clung
like a refugee to the sideboard.

David brought us over to look at the birds,
his basement converted into an aviary — everywhere
red, blue, yellow feathers, more exotic than
the Red Rose tea card variety.
Suddenly his father stamped down the stairs,
"What have I told you about having people over?"
Slapped his son, knocking his glasses from his face.
David cowered against the wire cage,
blood trickling from his nose.

The fathers were angry or silent.
Mr. Knight, handsome like Ronald Colman,
worked as a mechanic or gardener.
He suffered shell shock, never spoke of the war;
his fingers planted gladioli bulbs in the black earth.

The strangest father was Mr. Vogel.
His house was a house of secrets.
His boot filled with blood, he had limped miles
to surrender to the Allies.
Sometimes he looked at us with eyes
colder than the cobalt of a rifle barrel,
other times his eyes were those of a wounded animal
— a man who no longer knew his country.
His children swore at him in a foreign tongue
and he went to work unnoticed.

The Lost Glove

For my ninth birthday I get a red first-base glove
— not red, more maroon. Moulding the pocket to my hand,
I make fantastic catches in the Melody Road schoolyard.
The spring after we move I can't find it anywhere;
I forage rooms, trunks, the attic, wanting it to turn up
like a forgotten uncle, or a lost cousin.
There's a rumour Lacey threw it into the pond
at the bottom of Habitant Drive. I dream
of rescuing it from the sludgy, turbid depths.

The baseball summer passes without a glove.
Yellow bulldozers plow over the pond.
One day, Lacey confesses defiantly.
Against the railing I push him. I want to punch him,
as he whines in his contemptuous voice;
his ugly mother presses against the windowpane yelling,
"Leave him alone, what's he done to you!"
"He stole my glove." He cowers in the cold wind.
I grab him by the neck, and let him go...

This icy morning I think of that glove
moulded to my hand, that maroon glove
marooned deep in the earth — strange leather flower,
scarlet heart folded on its interlaced side.
The glove lost deep in layered glacial sand and gravel
becoming the colour of the earth, and the ink —
my own name slowly dissolving into the earth.

Scoutmaster

He taught us the national anthem;
it was hard to hear his words,
his face stitched with pink zippers,
barbed wire fences sewn across burned hills.
He'd fought hand to hand with a German soldier
whom he killed, then caught shrapnel.

Winter, he took us on a long trek
through Black Creek Conservation Area.
He divided us into two groups,
which we named Allies and Germans;
each imagined the other as German.

For hours we trekked,
searched for signs in the snow —
the broken twig,
the lost Mars Bar
breathing in the quiet,
reading the snow
for signs of violence.
Silence became voice.
Down through brambles
we moved into the battle
for our northern country.

I don't know how long
we climbed the hills, wading
waist high through drifts, looking
for the elusive enemy
over crests of snow, descending
tangled brush toward black water, pushing
aside wiry fences,
waiting for the sniper's shot,
the wound
            blood dripping in the snow
— *You're dead.*

Although we saw signs,
we never caught each other.
The cold was the enemy:
the wind on the face, the freezing feet.
Finally, we broke camp
at the meeting place,
got the fire going
as kid soldiers leaned on trunks,
socks hanging on branches like dead birds.

"In the game of concentration," he said,
"you have thirty seconds to remember
all the things on the table,
pen... rope... compass... apple... knife..."

He ordered us into lines.
We gathered utensils, canteens, walking sticks
for the homeward march, breaking
into his repertoire of army songs,
Pack up your troubles in your old kit bag...
Mademoiselle from Armentières, parlez-vous?
Marching through the drifting snow
we heard his voice call "Remember."

High School of Montreal

In the mural Jacques Cartier
presents gifts to the Indians.
The tarnished plaques were inscribed
when Greek and Latin were taught
and Phoebus' steeds reigned
with Victorian decorum
and dancers danced around Athena.
After the Somme and Vimy Ridge
the bronze boys were engraved
outside the office door.

A bell rings and children
spill out of classrooms —
Europe, China, Africa —
run beneath headless angels,
break into the library,
scramble beneath the portrait
of the headmistress
and scribble their desires
on classic pages.

Beyond the circulation desk
the librarian reads "Sweetness and Light,"
recalls Brooklyn's blue nights.
Johnny ransacks the paintings —
Botticelli, Rubens, Manet, Renoir —
searching for the naked women.

The librarian lights another cigarette,
looks toward Mount Royal gleaming in the sun.

Piano Lessons

Sitting down at my electric keyboard
I am Victor Borge of the morning
or Luis Borges alive in this storm of words.
Come let us compose the morning
where no groundhog will ever miss his shadow,
but go underground until well beyond
Saint Valentine's Day and movie massacres.
    And now
            there's music in the pines,
but suddenly I'm back in my grade nine typing class.

Miss Isabel Belopolsky, enchantress of
A Thousand and One High School Nights,
held my fingers arched high above
those unknown keys and suggested,
"You have fine fingers for the piano,"
then gave me the lowest
            typing mark in the history of Emery.
A mad secretarial conductor, she held the cane,
decoded the alphabet in coloured combinations
of the chemical table of elements.

There thirty-three future secretaries
punched out futures with the precision
of medical formulae:
"ASDF and now HJKL and WERT and UIOP."
Doctor Seuss combinations we used again and again.
"Dog sat on the cat."
"Man ran on the moon."
The bells in the room gone wild, "Night on Bald Mountain."
"Don't look at your fingers — look straight ahead."
A Panzer division we were driven
into the oblivion of the desert morning.

Blacksmith

Looking for wheels for a go-cart, George and I ride
into Weston. Inside *Wilf's Cycle and Sports*,
we tread the worn wooden floors
old westerns with their sawdust smell,
and ask the owner about wheels:
"Maybe you should try the old guy round the corner."

Around the corner we slip,
step into a barn where an old man
stands before a blazing forge,
a thin aged Vulcan in a shiny black apron,
the last blacksmith in Weston.

"Do you know where we can get some wheels?"
— hoping he has some lying among
the old harnesses and broken carriages.
He speaks to two eleven-year-old boys who've
stumbled into their adolescent twilight zone.
"I could make you a wheel, but it'd cost you
more than it's worth."

We see meadows beyond the darkness of his eyes,
and step carefully out of the barn
into the dull day where light breathes
suddenly from clouds, and the town lies still
like a museum where wires, railway ties
and roads stitch the world together.

Milkweed

A thirteen-year-old boy in the ravine lifts
the milkweed pod through a mauve
November sky upward,
releases seeds to the moon.
   This weed, no flower, no jack-in-the-pulpit,
but rough skin, nodules,
  bumps, hard metacarpal,
   faded puce, mole fur, velvet-ridged,
    ... a broken boat.
Once in public school we drew the pod
until it became a thousand things:
a clown striped banana,
a green beaked parrot perched in the wind,
or a mouth opening —
something forbidden, soft down skin.
   And its seeds, no seeds:
the silk inside no weed,
but softer than petals,
delicate Japanese prints.
The pod breaks open, launches seeds:
Irish Christmas tree hummingbird's tail
under comet-blue light
graceful grandmother's hair
Gayle's platinum hair blown about in the wind
circles dance, rise, spin and drop jazzy rhythms
words... rising... rushing...
     spread visibly the sun-scored air:
  domestic sputniks,
playful gyroscopes
   drifting stars.
Thirteen, I flip open the coarse green-tufted skin
among tall frosted grass and November twilight;
   they float up a ladder of lace,
 space pods
   spiralling through the mist
     toward the moon —
  their own milky way.

Relics

Propriété Privée, défense de passé.
We push open the saloon doors
into the cabin, great stone walls intact;
pans, like helmets, rot in the dust.

In woods, bottles stick through ice —
clear decanters, pink Revlon glass, Gatuso jars.
Search the rust and jewelled fragments...
    You are eight, push sand aside to find Egyptian vase,
hieroglyphs of wild birds, slaves and Pharaohs.
    You are ten, check the wavering tents,
Wasaga Beach, the lost doubloons in the sand.

Pry emerald loose, bone from icy shoal.
Push apart limbs among dazzling ice...
Broken bottles sink into the earth;
moss tongues curl around smooth bellies,
no maple syrup cans, only Javex glass.
Somewhere, huzza of hydroplane or buzz saw —
there in the bushes a crushed fuselage
corroded cone and shredded tire
a crumpled Cessna —
                the last maple syrup tank.
Vines coil around it,
the hydra dragging it slowly underground.

Cold shadows grow over
giant blocks of a still Gothic barn
where horses, unharnessed for the night,
breathed fiery breath into violet air.
Now broken stagecoach rim,
a lost sundial, leans against a trunk.
Kneeling I find
the great rusted femurs
      the sand-papered ribs
thick bolted teeth
fine line of the jaw
    — the maple sled just as it stopped running,
the bright invisible growth everywhere.

BURNT ISLAND LAKE

Burnt Island Lake

1

Nowhere to land. All campsites filled.
I hold the fatigued paddle.
Open water we race against declining light.
Ahead triangular shape, rock or tent.
No, only barren shore: twisted roots,
blasted trees, forbidden place.

2

Dark hills gather crimson bloodlight.
I jump into cool violet water,
swim over fish-shaped rocks and trunks;
beak of branch speaks water tongue.
Roots swirl out of stone legends,
Laocoön and his sons strangled by serpents;
bison sockets glare out of waves.

In night's blue geometry
stars pulse beyond Algonquin hills.
Things speak: the forest waves
to rhythm of wind and water;
I sit on the rim of the rocks
watch firelight dance over waves,
watch fire flow up through the rock bowl
as anger rises from darker caves.
The lonely raven's cry
and the raw laughter of loons
ring through lost mythologies
of Burnt Island Lake.

3

All night listen to the fire
listen to the cardiac rhythm of the waves
listen to the bears crawling,
raccoons scavenging, the forests walking,
the psychic fires singing.

A nomad, I came to these broken shores,
shattered roots. Trees cry,
it is in your ruins you find pain;
make your words sing
among twisted branches and cold currents,
forging your life, bringing you closer
                  to the voices of the earth.

Minerals

You looked at them,
but never named them.
Now your skin is shaped to rock
as water splashes around you.
You grew up among these rocks,
great eccentric shapes lining northern highways.
Every summer men drilled in pneumatic haze
splitting open the earth's surface.

Now you name them: pink granite, feldspar,
mica, hornblende and brown smoky quartz,
read them as musical notation.
You uncover rocks millions of years old.
Crystals grew out of the pistils of fire;
flames flowed in rivers of lava.

Now mica net sparkles in the frozen river
and rocks ripple as the muscle of the forearm.
Once these minerals flowed through crust
where stars exploded into supernova
then cooled to permanent petals of stone.
After millennia of slow motion pictures,
you hold them still in the form of your palm.

Still in this circus of colour you search
for the minerals the rocks contain.
Consider the processes of the world
how you name, feel and consume
these hybrid minerals of your body
— jewels you wear on your skin, on your heart.
Look how they reflect you,
how you become the elements of the earth.

Spoon

To practice poems
hold the spoon
feel the weight of the metal
on your fingertips,
the way the bubble
shows the carpenter
the level of the line.
To practice poems
try to ignore the noises of children
(you cannot ignore the children's noises)
but hold the spoon
(your son is also looking for a spoon).
Look at its lines
how well they are shaped
to its tapered form
the long neck opening out into the elliptical head.
Observe how the lines
circle the metal like natural striations
formed not of the earth
but the movement of the mouth
and fingers upon it.
Observe the peculiar colour
of rust and silver;
ignore the crests and words
(although you cannot fail to see
this is an Irish hotel with a Royal Crown crest
on opposite sides).
To practice poems
you must hold the spoon
more consciously than you would a pen;
feel its form and its smooth function.

Observe, too, how the form is not of the earth
but transformed from the metal out of the earth
deep fires, millions of years before.
If you want to practice poems
put the spoon into your mouth,
feel your lips around it:
sounds, shapes, textures, flavours.
Feel how it nourishes you
with its meats, vegetables and fruit,
how it takes them from the earth into you.

The Weight

"Don't overdress words."
You hold up spare hands —
the anatomy of pain.
There is no fat,
only stark muscle lines,
the frame of a boat
raised in dull gold light.
It is not pain, but fear
of not being yourself,
and not using these again.
You raise your legs up,
rub them the way
a carpenter rubs wood.
Through glasses into darkness
you look and weigh your words,
"This is what you must do,
just like this."

Stripping

From shelves strip away the years
five coats — white, green, red...
painted before the last world war.
Sanding, you release
first scent of tree,
whiff of forest,
lines of the wood.

Grain is wild wheat texture,
rich brown circles, structure
muscular and musical,
dark striations,
resinous capillaries.

Beneath blade, palms sweat,
older wood patterns unfold
the way words come.
You rub rich oil, wood lines,
find hue, colour and shape
unique as map lines,
original as fingerprints.

Soon shelves will hold
other leaves, maps, lines.
Revise the form of nature,
peel away surface years,
push and scrape until
you bring back wood,
sand until ribbed waves
under your hands shine.

Night Vision

Walking out to the log cabin for firewood
I gaze toward the great curved screen of sky
to see the Big Dipper
              then cast my eyes further afield
to the Little Dipper,
          and right above my head
the warrior with his studded buckle,
       the first time I've seen these together.
But there beyond the silo on the horizon —
a fire. Is the farmhouse burning
or is it an orange volcanic bubble,
an alien planet come suddenly into our orbit?
No, it's only the slow rising moon
           (sixty-eight miles per second)
throwing its light over this cold snowscape
just beyond the tower and the branches
— exotic orange, this impossible poem
I want to write.
     And I run across the snow to bring
you half-naked and shivering in your dressing gown
to look upon this wildly improbable moon.

Ultrasound

Sitting in the waiting room
I scan the puzzles of paintings, thinking of child
and gaze at the shifting perspectives of Escher,
Chagall's childhood horses and chickens
swirling through a turbulence of colour.

Now scanning the screen I try to get
a perspective on it. The doctor divines the fetal form;
you make your appearance on black and white TV
floating between the pelvic fissures of the earth,
your protozoan body swimming beyond our machines
through the coloured inner rivers.

Alien space explorers, we probe dark depths
where star child you glimmer
within the grey possibilities of mother;
your heart pumps luminously in underwater breathing.
Amphibian, you are paddling through the underworld.
I see you for the first time, phantom child.

And the day you were born
    the most beautiful yellow bird
        sang from our plum tree.

Hippocrates in the Pharmacy

A blue transparent cranium
bust of modern man
absorbs light from medical paraphernalia.
Smooth plastic features offer
an illusion of peering into the mind,
yet reflect only more blue,
tropical Laurentian ink
or Caribbean poster seas,
lovers kissing in ultramarine waters.

The transparency, blue
as thought itself,
shines in Arctic clarity
revealing nothing,
            the nothing that is.

Hippocrates swore allegiance to Apollo,
not this android stare
which sees man denuded of himself
surrounded by medicine for every ailment
not blessed by the gods of health.
I remember the Greek busts
when stone became skin, and wisdom
spoke through craggy cheeks and rough-hewn brows.

Circle the modern transparent mind
that attracts itself by a reflection of itself.
Look beyond the uneven scales of justice
to the poster boys in dark glasses
smiling with the blindness of style.

The Glass Blower

Beyond his shoulder horses run;
he breathes flame into glass,
moulds the air into clear forms,
original as the first time I saw television
where hands modelled the animals of Genesis.

Poised in the centre of the spellbound crowd
he casts his material in a sleight of hand,
his eyes charged with a cosmic gaiety
as he exhales glass into musical form:
fine tubes, soft angles and treble clefs.

An animal tamer, he draws shapes
out of the wilderness into the barely animal.
In the glass-roofed coliseum, beyond the hushed crowd,
the equestrians ride roughly over the hard earth.

Strangely clear through mist I see
this sensual alchemist shape lines
into coils of honey and amber globes
making glass properties into gold.

With light flourishing gestures
he inspires perfect rhythms,
readies the audience for the flames of colour
as his lips blow glass into forms,
precise as a French horn player's notes.

These are no blue souvenir lions,
no frozen tiger-angelfish,
but light, form and energy;
his eyes flash as he breathes fire into glass,
                    the horses in the coliseum running.

DARK WINDOWS

The Shape of the Earth

Here the earth curves before our eyes —
rolls away, down toward clear horizons.

Here the earth is rich in cold black forms,
rolls to the movement of the hip and thigh.

And here it strikes your eye as a page
as you write upon it now in new forms.

These plants and trees become words,
the hills and ponds, the heart and eyes.

The land is new in this strange light
where city no longer holds,

but you stand alone before the horizon and
the light sounds above the earth

in the clarity of a chime. And you write upon
the wide earth under the silver span of

sky, over the rolling land where now
you feel the rim of the circle

and the power of the line.

The Cup

Steam rises from the cup,
hieroglyphics in the air,
shadows on a golden page.

Steam rises from dark coffee,
mist from a still lake —
shadow across mountain slope.

Look before you drink,
blue-gold ideograms
painted on porcelain.

Figures of life:
house   man   woman   child

Sunlight on the beach —
this morning, drink this coffee,
drink the world.

Silence

To be in touch with things
mist bathes the coasts of the world.

Should I type tonight,
cause the Chinese man to waken.

Upstairs a boy cries out from a nightmare;
his Japanese mother slips out of bed.

Soon she will stand before the waterfall
in the rock gardens of Kyoto.

The little boy will say hello
to the ancient guard of the gate.

My typewriter is a silent temple,
blue mist drifting across a distant shore.

Path at Twilight

These days twilight is early;
darkness creeps upon us.

Through cold, calm air we
glide; beyond wire fences

houses are empty. Here
earth is close and we walk

not on concrete, but on roots:
striations, knots, vessels.

Driftwood they break
the earth. Sky aquamarine,

sunbars glisten on grey clouds,
and the moon, a sloop, sails.

Foreigner

I know the curves of your body
like a familiar country.
Now that you are gone
I am foreigner.

Blackout

Outside the city is captured in freeze frame. This moment is held in the silence of the silver screen. Orange leaves are suspended in crystal; the boughs are black in silicon transparency, and the streets glazed in treachery. Here the world is beautiful and dangerous as branches break the circuits and ice pellets nick cars and passengers.

Here the world is silver; the machine is broken and we must sit by dark windows again. Yet there is a beauty in all of this — I mean in the immobility. We don't have to report to work or school, but can sit through the day and enjoy events.

However, night is a different story. The city is given over to darkness. I venture out through the blackened streets lighted only by yellow flares. The houses are lonely and fragile, crouched in larger shadows. Here people venture out of need, to clear a path, to buy candles.

Here men and women try to get out of where they are. Blackout. Notions. Shapes. Tyrannosaurian plow. Darkness, primitive men wandering around caves with nuclear fear, searching for fire. More likely, it's the actual fear that one has had in Belfast, Beirut, or anywhere — close to what we could be. Here and there boys with sticks swipe at ice-knives, nomads wandering in darkness...

Mountain Walk

Behind me the lovers sit in their relic cars as I stand above the shoal, listen to the surf break over subterranean life. On this primordial shore the land slowly rises from the dolphin-blue, and amphibians crawl through the snowy tide. Wind sweeps through tentacles of this coral sea among intimate lost voices.

Through the blurred pines I climb toward the peak of lights — the four moons of Jupiter. Before me a violet aura hums, while behind dim lanterns crackle from the lower circle of hell. I climb higher where a column of neon lights, a double cross shines over emulsified snow. There is no one.

As I trek, rain pellets crack the snow in unknown codes. I look for signs, try to humanize this landscape with words, but there is only the wind speaking in dumb tones. The black branches are twisted girders, melted iron, torn cables. And the trees. What are they? Wounded soldiers speaking of their death, shamans chanting their prophecies from bags of lost herbs.

Where is the chalet? In the distance three lamps glow. There is the mausoleum: the dead windows, the grotesque mouth, the rooms of policies. The path leads to a lifeless arena, an empty proscenium. No stairs. There, a flagless pole, outspread tablets I cannot decipher, a row of empty tripods. Eerie light hovers over frozen cairns, hulks and the shapes of bodies. Down in the mist an aqueous eye stares at me. The wind whines through the red earth.

Snow

Are there not treasures in the snow? It awakens me to colour and forms a bright context out of its anonymity. Beneath its smooth surface I see idiosyncrasies: microprisms breaking into chromatic scales... myriad globes glowing... glacial spores blossoming...

What I love is the mathematical precision with which it covers the earth in frozen solutions. As I walk across the tabula rasa, deeper into the shifting planes, there is a geometric excitement: fine logarithms, musical phrases, a wonderful amnesia. Snowflakes, words tumble — changing infinities in fin-like speed. New possibilities whirl out of violet haloes and the Milky Way.

Snow paradise. Carousels of evening horns and bells. You cover everything in a philosophical eloquence, a great white alibi.

Rain

There are days like today when all I want is rain. Rain, the rich paradox, has a misty clarity continually transforming light and shape. Rain makes me feel the presence of that light — the presence of the sea. It makes me aware of perspective: I look out into the day's mirror and it replies, "no, there isn't much." It's the clear days that throw me for a loop, trying to watch a lush picture in a gallery from a great distance. I appreciate the parables that rain provides: the son who shot up his house because his mother turned back the clocks so that he missed his employment interview.

In this darkening twilight, riding the shuttle bus, I am in love with all rainy days, ambiguous and naked like forgotten lovers. Words breathe upon the windowpane. I can just make out the chaotic traffic... the work camps... the spaceway... the Christmas tree... Picasso's and the erotic floor show in the heavens... and there in the clouds floats an orange bar, a de Kooning...

It is this moist suspension that I spin on through the rain, the synchronization of the swimmer as he breaks the waves. In this tangible silence I glide through the twilight trajectory, toward the dark comfortable place I name home.

Midnight

My favourite hour. How comfortable to sit here listening to the refrigerator humming, the syncopation of the clock, the midnight bus breaking: the warming up of an orchestra.

After a day's long journey I reach the shore and look out on sleep's dark breakers. Today we painted a wall — not much, mind you — but those old green flowers are finally gone. We can hang pictures *there*. But to get back to midnight, not the beach, but the wide red table that spreads before me like a mesa. In the landscape are walnuts, green grapes, Spiderman and wooden Russian dolls. My thought stops. I step outside myself. I am the stranger walking by the sea.

Midnight, my favourite hour, when the refrigerator is an Arctic piano. After the hockey game last night, I drove out into the unrecognizable mauve city. On the mountain's edge the boy and girl drank, danced, sang into the wind.

On the edge be near the power, not the guardian of thought. Be the stranger, the reader. Come, the scherzo is over. Already the drum of the clock is fading and the piano plays softly like a cardiogram. Listen, the late night bus revellers, the voices of sleep. The clock steps draw you closer to the waves. Fatigue, like a friend, takes you into the weird night, childhood. Now after travelling all day, relearn the world. Stranger, the sea is here. Forget and welcome.